Dedication

To Daniel,
who always tries his best
and never gives up

Acknowledgments

I wish to thank Meredith Johnson, whose charming illustrations resonate so well with the text, and Marieka Heinlen for the exuberant design. I appreciate Judy Galbraith and the entire Free Spirit family for their dedicated support of the series. I am especially grateful to Margie Lisovskis for her diplomatic style as well as her talented editing. I also recognize Mary Jane Weiss, Ph.D., for her expertise and gift in teaching social skills. Lastly, these books have been inspired by my children—especially Andrea, age six, as I have viewed life through her wise and innocent eyes.

There are lots of things I want to try.

Some things are easy for me.

Some things are harder.

I might need to practice over and over.

I can try something new.

I might like it!

It's fun to try new things.

If something seems hard at first,
I like to imagine myself doing it.

If something isn't going well,
I might try it a new way . . .

or take a break and
try again later . . .

or just try a little longer.

It's okay when I make mistakes.
I learn by trying.

It helps to remember things
I already do well.

When something doesn't work out,
I may want to quit.

I can take a big breath and stay calm.
And I can remind myself to stick with it.

When I finish what I start,
people see that they can depend on me.

This helps us get along.

I learn from people who don't give up even when something is hard.

They keep at it until they finish
or until they can do it well.

Learning about other people who stick with something

can give me the courage to keep trying.

I know people who encourage me.

They're happy for me
when I do something new.

I might ask for a little help,
and do the rest by myself.

Each day I can do my best.

Something I do might even help someone else.

When I work hard at something,

I get better at it and it seems easier.

If I try something new and stick with it,
I'll find out what I like

and what I can do.

Ways to Reinforce the Ideas in *Try and Stick with It*

Try and Stick with It teaches *perseverance,* a process that helps children develop assertiveness, courage, patience, determination, and persistence. If you wish, explain the term *persevere* to children: to keep practicing and working at something until you can do it. Here is a quick summary of perseverance skills, most of which are mentioned in the children's text:

1. Decide to finish what you start.
2. Imagine yourself doing it.
3. Learn about how other people do it.
4. Remember things you already do well.
5. Try it a new way.
6. Take a break and try again later.
7. Try a little bit longer.
8. Learn from mistakes you make while trying.
9. Take a deep breath.
10. Remind yourself to stick with it.
11. Do it one step at a time.
12. Ask for help if you need it.

As you read each page spread, ask children:

- What's happening in this picture?

Here are additional questions you might discuss, referring to the list of skills above as needed:

Pages 1–3
- What are some things this boy might want to try?
- What things are easy for you? Were they ever hard? Why are they easy now?

Pages 4–5
- What is the boy trying to learn? Will it take lots of practice?
- What are some other things that need lots of practice?

Pages 6–7
- Have you ever tried something even though you didn't think you'd like it? What happened?

Pages 8–11
- Why is it sometimes hard to learn something new? *(Responses might include: "It might take a lot of time." "I might get hurt." "I might not like it.")*
- What does it mean to imagine? *(Children may suggest pretending or the idea of "make believe." It might be helpful to talk in terms of "picturing yourself" or "making a picture in your head.")* What is something you can imagine (picture) yourself doing now? when you're older?

Pages 12–15

- How can you help yourself keep trying? *(Ideas might include trying a new way, taking a break and trying again, trying a little longer, remembering things you already do well.)* How will that help?
- What can you tell yourself the next time something is hard? *(Encourage all reasonable responses. Some answers might include: "I can do it if I keep trying." "It will be fun once I know how to do it." "I can ask for help if I need it." "It's okay to make a mistake.")*

Pages 16–19

- Have you ever wanted to quit because something was really hard? What happened?
- Why is it important to keep trying?
- Who depends on you to finish what you start? Who knows you'll stick with it?
- How does sticking with something help you get along with other people? *(Other people are happy when they know they can count on you to do what you say you'll do and finish what you start. It's nice to be able to count on other people, too.)*

Pages 20–25

- Do you know (know about) someone who tried hard to do something? What did the person learn to do? Do you think it was hard?
- Who can help you when something's hard?

Pages 26–31

- What is something you can help other people do? How did you learn to do that?
- *(point to featured boy)* What did the boy learn to do? How did he learn?
- What is something you worked hard to be able to do? How did you learn to do it?
- What is something you haven't tried that you would like to try?
- What is something you want to be able to do someday?

Perseverance Games

Read this book often with your child or group of children. Once children are familiar with the book, refer to it when teachable moments arise involving both positive behavior and problems related to trying new things and persevering. In addition, use the following activities to reinforce children's understanding of how to try something new or difficult and stick with it (adapting them as needed for use with a single child):

Tortoise and Hare Game

Materials: Sheet of cardstock at least 11" x 14", marker, 8 or more stickers (such as stars), pictures of a tortoise and a hare (drawn or cut from a magazine or clip art), glue, index cards, one standard die, game tokens for up to 4 players (such as different buttons, one per player); optional—copy of the story "The Tortoise and the Hare" from *Aesop's Fables*

Preparation: With the marker, make a gameboard by drawing a horseshoe-shaped sidewalk on the cardstock, marking off at least 30 spaces. Write "Start" and "Finish" at the ends and glue the pictures of the tortoise and hare at the "Start" square. Put a sticker on 8 or more spaces. Then, on index cards, write individual scenarios similar to those in the samples on page 34.

Directions: Before playing the game, read and/or talk about the fable where the tortoise persisted and won the race even though the hare was faster. To play the game, a child rolls the die and moves the appointed number of squares. When landing on a space that has a sticker, the child draws a card, reads it, and decides whether the person in the scenario kept trying. Then the child rolls the die again and moves the appointed number of spaces, going forward if the scenario showed perseverance or backward if it did not. Play until each player crosses the finish line (like the tortoise!).

Sample Scenarios:

- Alexis got back on her bike after she fell.
- Fredo made another picture after he spilled all over his first one.
- Joshua's dad said he could play after he cleaned his room, but Joshua was too tired to clean it.
- Kelsey said she wouldn't go back to school after the first day.
- Ari was having trouble learning to tie his shoes, so he hid them under the bed and wore a pair that didn't have laces instead.
- Serena kept practicing her reading even though her brother teased her about it.
- Ty finished his school assignment before watching TV.
- It took Chantel three nights to finish a note to send her grandfather.

"Stick with It" Role Plays

Use the scenario cards from the previous activity; make additional cards if you wish, and place the cards in an envelope. Have a child draw a card from the envelope. Read it and ask, "Is this child trying hard? Is (she/he) sticking with it?" If the answer is yes, have children act out the scenario. If the answer is no, ask, "How could the child keep trying?" Refer to the skills on page 32 as needed. Invite children to act out ways the child could try and stick with it.

Perseverance Pictures

Materials: Magazines, large index cards, scissors, glue, drawing paper, crayons or markers

Preparation: Cut out pictures from magazines that show people involved in activities requiring perseverance. Glue the pictures to large index cards.

Directions: Place the cards in a stack facedown and invite a child to draw a card. Ask, "What's happening?" Then ask, "How do you think the person learned to do this?" Discuss different ways the person might have kept trying when things were hard or weren't going well. After discussing several cards, have children draw pictures about working hard to be able to do something. They might base their pictures on any of the cards discussed or on their own experiences. At the bottom of the pictures, have children write (or dictate for you to write) a sentence describing how the person in the drawing persevered.

Stories About People Who Kept Trying

Ask children to learn a story about a parent, relative, ancestor, teacher, or friend who worked hard to accomplish something even though it was difficult. Invite children to report their stories. Discuss how the people kept trying and working to do what they did. Ask questions such as, "How did the person learn to do that?" "Why was it hard?" "How did the person feel when things didn't go well?" "What did the person do to keep going?" "Can you imagine doing that, too?"

"We Keep Trying" Posters

Ask children what they would say to encourage someone who wanted to quit trying. Write down children's ideas. Then have children make posters that encourage everyone to try and stick with things that are difficult. Phrases might include "Hang in There," "Never Give Up," "Stick with It," "Keep at It," and "Give It Your All." Have or help children write the slogans on their posters and then decorate the posters. Display the posters and refer to them in situations that call for perseverance.

Other Suggestions for Helping Children Persevere

Use a goal chart. Help a child choose a goal to work on, such as independence in getting ready for school or bedtime, doing chores at home, or completing tasks or assignments for school. Talk together about the specific goal and strategies for working to accomplish it. Make a chart for reaching the goal and put it in a prominent place. Have the child put a sticker on the chart each time he or she works on the goal. Decide on small rewards to mark both progress and persistence.

Help children find role models. Role models can be famous people, people from history, and people (young and old) who are closer to children as well. Read books and talk about people—past and present—who have persisted in spite of challenges. (You'll find many biographies for children at the library. Also check Web sites such as *www.myhero.com* and *www.giraffe.org* for profiles and teaching ideas to use with children.) Discuss questions like, "What did this person do to keep trying?" and, "What would have happened if the person didn't keep trying?" Also invite friends and community members into your home or classroom to share with children how they tried and kept working to succeed at something. Encourage children to be role models for others, too: "Jeremy, can you tell us how you finally found a way to keep the block tower from tipping?" "Katja, how many times did you fall off the pogo stick before you figured out how to use it?"

The Free Spirit **Learning to Get Along**® Series

For ages 4–8. *Each $10.95; 40 pp.; softcover; color illus.; 9" x 9"*

Listen and Learn
by Cheri J. Meiners, M.Ed.
Knowing how to listen is essential to learning, growing, and getting along with others. This book helps children develop skills for listening, understand why it's important to listen, and recognize the positive results of listening. Includes suggestions for reinforcing the skills being taught.

When I Feel Afraid
by Cheri J. Meiners, M.Ed.
Children today have many fears, both real and imagined. Even young children can learn basic coping skills. Encouraging words and supportive illustrations guide children to face their fears and know where to turn for help. Little ones also learn simple ways to help themselves. Includes ideas for supporting children when they feel afraid and a list of resources.

Share and Take Turns
by Cheri J. Meiners, M.Ed.
Sharing is a social skill all children need to learn—the earlier the better. This book helps children practice sharing, understand how and why to share, and realize the benefits of sharing. Includes questions to prompt discussion and games to play.

Respect and Take Care of Things
by Cheri J. Meiners, M.Ed.
Respect, responsibility, and stewardship are concepts that even young children can relate to—because they have things they value. This book encourages children to pick up after themselves, put things back where they belong, and ask permission to use things that don't belong to them. It also teaches simple environmental awareness: respecting and taking care of the earth. Includes ideas for adult-led activities and discussions.

Join In and Play
by Cheri J. Meiners, M.Ed.
It's fun to make friends and play with others, but children have to make an effort, and they have to know the rules—like ask before joining in, take turns, play fair, and be a good sport. This book teaches the basics of cooperation, getting along, making friends, and being a friend—skills every child wants and needs. Includes ideas for games adults can use with kids to reinforce the skills being taught.

Be Polite and Kind
by Cheri J. Meiners, M.Ed.
Politeness helps people get along. When children are courteous, respectful, and kind, other people enjoy being around them. This book teaches the basics of good manners and gracious behavior. Children learn the importance of saying "Please," "Thank you," "You're welcome," "Excuse me," and "I'm sorry." They begin to see the benefits that courtesy brings. Scenarios and role-play activities help adults reinforce the book's lessons.

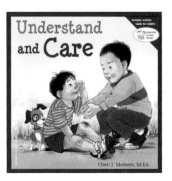

Understand and Care
by Cheri J. Meiners, M.Ed.
Friendly and engaging, this book encourages children to listen to and respect the feelings of those around them. Examples of positive interaction combine with child-friendly language to help children develop empathy and understanding. Also includes a special section for adults with discussion questions, ideas, and empathy games.

To place an order or to request a free catalog of SELF-HELP FOR KIDS®
and SELF-HELP FOR TEENS® *materials, please write, call, email,*
or visit our Web site:

Free Spirit Publishing Inc.
217 Fifth Avenue North • Suite 200 • Minneapolis, MN 55401
toll-free 800.735.7323 • local 612.338.2068
fax 612.337.5050 • help4kids@freespirit.com
www.freespirit.com